GW01425147

Some Rhymes

Frank Beck

ISBN 978-1-291-88221-6

Contents

A walk on the Heath

The highest flag in London flies
Between the Whitestone pond and skies
With homes of elegance surrounded
On every side by nature bounded

Burgeoning life in sight and sound
Cocooned with pleasantness all round
Birds fly and insects hover there
One feels that spring is in the air

The bus that brought me drives away
And leaves me with an idle day
Drawn by the greenery beneath
I start my walk on Hampstead Heath

I say a walk; a pleasing ramble
It's really more an awkward scramble
No time to contemplate the view
When there are rocks and potholes too

The path now levels; there's a place
To contemplate surrounding space
Mother and child go for a walk
Two lovers are engaged in talk

And all around the flowers bloom
The new-sprung heather and the broom
And there ahead just yards below
Some houses through the bushes show

The Vale of Health – a curious name,
The explanations are the same
Was it the waters that were there?
Does it refer to plague-free air?

Whichever history you give
An enviable place to live
This hamlet which you find by stealth
Breathes comfort, beauty, pride in wealth

Rest? No. I will continue down
In the direction of the town
The scenery I spy beneath
Is now more park and lawn than heath

With seats for resting by the grass
And paths quite wide enough to pass
Some things to see, a fallen log
A lone man promenading dog

And suddenly I look below
What does the far horizon show?
Blue sky with billows clean and white
And under that a stirring sight

There is Saint Paul's, the London Eye
Natwest and Gherkin pierce the sky
With all the beauty I can see
I think they built it just for me.

Escape

Lie down, eyes closed, and then sleep tight
Dreaming's the pleasure of my night

By day my age is full four score
At night I'm only twenty four

By day I limp and drag my feet
At night I'm active and I'm fleet

By day I've a befuddled brain
At night it's twenty four again

By day I look at girls and wish
At night I score with every dish

I'm better off by night than day
I think I might decide to stay

How to write a poem

A dactylic foot
In a jingle you'd put

Iambs are used
When the writer's amused

And Trochees attached
When a joke's to be hatched

For a stanza that's witty and mordant and terse
Must never be written in unstructured verse

But when voicing a thought that is grave and profound
You should go for a grey and less colourful sound

For pensive constructions with deep meaning fraught
Blank verse is the medium for serious thought

So reserve all your pleasure with rhythms and rhymes
For trivial lines and less serious times

Poet's block

Tuesday bloody Tuesday
I must write another rhyme
I must get my act together
While there's still a little time

I know it needn't rhyme a lot
I know it needn't scan
That doesn't bother me a jot
Write poetry I can

A poem has to have a theme
A thing that it's about
It's seeking that which makes be scream
And weep and moan and shout

The laureate has a lighter task
He does it to command
He simply has his queen to ask
Or rather to demand:

"Write something for our birthday Sir
Or the wedding of our son
Or celebrate another war
That we have lost or won"

But if I think of something
I'll invest in it with verve
And write it oh so quickly
Before I lose my nerve

Magnolia tree

The seasons follow one by one
And spring arrives when winter's done
For then the old magnolia tree
Springs into life for all to see

The blossoms of a creamy white
Reflecting early April's light
The blooms resemble, on reflection
The rose, with even more perfection

But wait a while, another night
Will make the beauty extra right
And add improvement to the tree
Could the effect still better be?

I wake next day and look outside
I find perfection's been denied
For there below the canopy
Shed blossoms lie beneath the tree

And with regret I have to say
The tree was better yesterday
For when the peak has come to pass
You'll know there *was* no greener grass

An Oldie's complaint

The bell-shaped curve of doctor Gauss
Describes the life of man and mouse
He's born, he lives and then he dies
So it may come as no surprise
That many fail to stay alive
While others manage to survive

The trouble is – don't get me wrong
It's not all fun to live so long
For many of your bits may fail
And those that work will tend to ail
But worse than that the oldie tends
Progressively to lose his friends

And when your stories you recall
The new young friends don't care at all
For they'll consider you a bore
When you recount what's gone before
And all those things you learnt with pain
They'll simply have to learn again

Orderly retreat

The philosopher sees what we've all seen before
But unlike the rest of us sees a bit more
He discovers that what we considered as true
Is part of a concept that's different and new

Our previous knowledge considered it too
But this new result gives a different view
The problem is what was contained in the Books
Is quite inconsistent with how it now looks

Let's turn the thinker into a pariah
Call him a charlatan. Say he's a liar
That way the canon is fully intact
And quite unaffected by logic or fact

Many years later the thinker's forgotten
We all had agreed that his dogma was rotten
Only the merchants mechanics and hacks
Follow the heretic pioneer's tracks

Business flourishes, industry grows
And all this in spite of the fact that one knows
It's based on ideas that we knew all along
Were the work of a charlatan known to be wrong

The wealth and the comfort we plainly now see
Cannot be ignored by the powers that be
We'll have to allow that the thinker was right
Perhaps we should give up that part of the fight

We'll alter our angle on what's in the Book
Enough to allow us to get off the hook
Then we can go on believing it's true
And focus our strength on opposing the new

Osculation

Each man or woman has a face
Each feature has its proper place

Two eyes, a mouth, ears and a snout
Most are concave; the nose goes out

When they're engaged in seeking bliss
A pair will often want to kiss

For this one has to juxtapose
The mouths while disengaging nose

It can be done but takes some care
That's what defines a happy pair

A poet's tool kit

The first and most important part
Is have a plot before you start
For lacking plot there is no way
To write what you intend to say

Having decided to convey
This new idea you've had you may
Decide a structure for your verse
Go classical, you could do worse

Look in the book where you can choose
Iambs or trochees, structures whose
Rhythms regularly pound
To turn your best ideas to sound

Or you can opt to do without
A bold alternative, no doubt
To the commanding rhythmic beat
Resulting from these classic feet

Next is the problem of our time
Should we attempt to make it rhyme?
For here we swim in murky pools
Strong feelings from competing schools

Dramatic thoughts require prose
But otherwise, and failing those
You might do worse than make it rhyme
Though some may deem it quite a crime

And as you bask in sin infernal
You might make some of them internal
And as your work is out of date
You might as well alliterate

And if the publishers reject you
There's always some who will respect you
For if you slaved with all your might
It's likely that you've done it right

Smartphone Saga

I've just convinced myself that I am winning
When - oops the thing goes back to the beginning

I'm sure I touched the buttons right as told
Perhaps it's simply that I'm getting old

I dutifully listen to those chaps
Who tell me how to download useful apps

I know that you will think that it's absurd
But it's aware I'm not a fellow nerd

I'm perfectly convinced it knows it's me
And takes advantage when I'm all at sea

I'm sure that you'll consider me uncouth
But telephones were simpler in my youth

Socks

It's sad but true: here are the facts
My socks they come from Marks' in packs.
Not all the same, alas alack
Three colours feature in a pack
Then to the washer off they go
They go in pairs, is it not so?
And when they're dry, I sort them out
Two at a time, or thereabout.
It always fails, this simple trick
It very nearly makes me sick.
I'm ever of two socks bereft
An unmatched pair is always left!

To my barber

If you want to get a haircut
that is perfect fore and aft
Simply visit Vas and Marcos.
They are masters of their craft

The client feels important.
They treat him very well
And that's appreciated.
Quite a bonus, truth to tell

Some clients are obscure
and insignificant like us
But even the celebrities
are welcomed without fuss

So come to Vas and Marcos,
and get your haircut done
A necessary chore, that's true,
but why not also fun?

Chicken soup

Buy a large organic hen
Cut away the thighs and then
Use them afterwards for roasting
If you're single-person hosting

Cut and throw away the wings
Also parson's nose and things
Rid the body of its skin
Throw the skin into the bin

Put the meat into the pot
Vegetables add a lot
I prefer to favour four
Some use five or six or more.

Three large carrots, one big leek
One huge onion you should seek
(Failing that, of small ones two)
Celery is good for you

Break away three celery sticks
Add two soup cubes to the mix
Pepper salt and water too
Now your soup is set to stew

How much water? Not too long
If you like it rich and strong
Just enough to cover it
Makes a soup that's good and fit

Now you're finished with the toil
You can bring it to the boil
When it's ready you can tell
From the quite delicious smell

Citrus Drama

Prodigious choice I find is mine
Satsuma, orange, clementine
O what a quandary I'm in
Perhaps I'll have a mandarin

I pick it up; its shiny skin
Goes easily from fruit to bin
Inside the fresh and juicy meat
Gives promise of a luscious treat

A segment's broken off and slips
Quite pleasantly between my lips
Delicious flavours I detect
Linked to aromas most elect

But when that noble treat I swallow
I'm left with disappointment hollow
For as the juicy fruit I gulp
I'm conscious of a shred of pulp

O what predictable bad luck
Between two teeth that shred is stuck
I try to poke and suck and pick
But stubbornly that pulp will stick

The irritation drives me mad
It's disproportionately bad
It's even worse I find because
My bathroom's out of dental floss

I think of my Swiss Army knife
It's always there to save my life
It has a toothpick on one side
It works. Relief. I'm satisfied!

The Snail

The snail has feelers on his head
No toes, he has a foot instead
To cover him he has a shell
That keeps him safe and dry as well

The snail when he decides to roam
Is always furnished with a home
At night he doesn't need a nest
His hardy shell, it serves him best

Not male or female, yes, that's right
The snail is a hermaphrodite
And snails live singly, yes they do
Avoiding life as one of two

An easy life, devoid of fuss
And quite unlike the world of us
For humans, when they choose to roam
Prefer to do so from a home

And when returning to it late
They like a welcome from a mate
So let me park my shell with you
You might prefer that option too

Thoughts on English grammar

I'm feeling rather weak today
Think I'll lie down, or is it lay
For if it happened yesterday
I lay would be the thing to say

You lie with words or on a bed
Just use the transitive instead
But please avoid the use of lay
When lie is what you mean to say

For hens do laying with their eggs
And folk do it with other folk
And though each egg contains a yolk
To lie an egg is just a joke

Valentine 1

More a mollusc than a male
With resemblance to a snail

Slow but sure he wheedled in
Tempting her to live in sin

She was playing hard to get
Keeping him away, and yet

Who can stem the running tide
Human nature's on his side

The decision's grave and weighty
Very soon they'll both be eighty

Finally she had to choose
What's a woman got to lose?

Now we're settled well and fine
Darling, be my Valentine!

Valentine 2

Saint Valentine's a funny saint
Historical he surely aint
For with a wish to get it right
I googled him this very night

This Valentine, he's one of seven
Who have that special place in heaven
To whom their God had given breath
Only to take it back in death.

It happened on this very date
The public hoped to seal the fate
Of lovers, be they young and old
A rite of spring, or so I'm told

It seems that on the Appian way
Some Valentine was killed that day
Just as they sought a useful name
To link with lovers; what a shame

They thought they were so very clever
Lovers and Saint were linked forever
And that is why this hopeless bard
Today is sending you a card.

Valentine 3

Once a year I 'm told they do it
And they say there's nothing to it
Simply send a Valentine
"Guess who sent it? Please be mine"

Do such missives hit the spot?
I'd say definitely not
Bad relationship? Then mend it
Buy a card, address and send it

But the essence of the art
If you want to win her heart
Is to woo her every way
Say you love her every day

I'm not sending one this year
Though I love her, never fear
Valentines may be rejected
Constancy will be respected

Valentine 4

He lost his head in 269
His name of course was Valentine

To celebrate that happy day
All lovers have to make their way
To shops that deal in special cards
Embellished by atrocious bards

They write a jingle for each one
(Which is occasionally fun
If words are apt and rhythm slick)
If not they tend to make you sick

I wouldn't buy such rhymes for you
I'd make my own, and send them too
The wish *I* send you is sincere
So be my valentine my dear

Wisdom

Qualified by being eighty
You can make pronouncements weighty
Take more time to analyse
People think you're being wise

True, when you have lived so long
There's less chance of being wrong
Errors you remember making
Risks that you remember taking

Bad decisions that you've made
Penalties that you have paid
Things you said and then were sorry
Things you did that made you worry

When they ask for your advice
And they think they're being nice
Tell them what you really know
In an earnest voice that's slow

I can't help. You're on your own
My experience has shown
You have everything it takes
You must make your own mistakes

History of Inventions

I've got an idea! I've got an idea!
Just let me show you a sketch of it here
I really must show you and try to explain
So I don't go away and forget it again

Dear fellow you surely don't think that it's new
Or an idea that's freshly invented by you
It is really quite commonplace and what is more
Things like that have been made and exploited
before

Oh it's different you mean? Well it simply won't
go
I'm an expert dear friend, and so I should know
Besides there are too many gadgets like that
The thing you've invented is simply old hat

We've happily managed forever without it
We'll manage in future, no reason to doubt it
My opinion is this, and I think you should heed it
Your device is redundant and people don't need
it

***

Remember that gadget of some years ago?
It is now used by everyone. Thought you should
know
That idea! But it's obvious. Everyone knows
Any fool could have thought up and made one of
those!

Cherished Registrations

Many folk would go quite far
To buy a number for their car
Boring 94312
Being random, just won't do
No, the number must be fun
They'd like 54321

But they're simply all the same
No one wins this silly game
For the smallest ugly one
If you bought it, just for fun
Might be deemed the height of chic
Just because it is unique

Dotcom Shopping

No need to drive or park your car
You do your shop from where you are
No need to search or walk for miles
No tedious plod along the aisles

And when deciding on a choice
Of products, hear the silent voice
Of pictures showing what they've got
What choice? They have an awful lot

And when you've finished with your list
Ensuring that no item's missed
Just book a time you'd like your stuff
A short day's notice is enough

You simply type a secret number
And then you go away and slumber
There really is no way of stopping
The tide of this new style of shopping

But don't you miss the human touch
The random meetings, chats and such?
Sadly, when all is said and done
Shopping from home is far less fun

The hi-tech home

My home's agreeable enough
Such comfort needs a lot of stuff

A lot of stuff, you ask me, why?
To heat and cool, to wash and dry

Hi tech computers and the rest
Large screen TVs; I buy the best.

And when it's working like a dream
This well greased residence machine

I revel in its smooth success
Immersed in luxury, no less

But hear the burden of my song
From time to time one bit goes wrong

I try to mend the thing and then
I find I have to call some men

That causes cost and worry too
I hate technology, don't you?

All the news that's fit to print

The week's for work
Weekend's for play
I bought the Sunday Times today

It looks quite big
And very nice
And so it should. It's twice the price

I took it home, and I was able
To lay it out upon the table
The supplements and glossy mags
Sealed up by groups in plastic bags

The sections on a week in Rome
And those on profit from your home
The section on designer clothes
I soon got to dispose of those

And gardening and classic cars
And drinks in fashionable bars
Prize winning books and "What is in"
Were all selected for the bin

And what was left? A sheet or two
Much less than when the thing was new
This is the Sunday Times I bought
I'll look more carefully, I thought

Whole pages of commercial patter
Conceal the journalistic matter
Some gossip on a politician
How paedophiles now face perdition

And how a bland and healthy diet
Makes you live longer if you try it.
Ah silly me, I really thought
The latest news is what I'd bought

Technological Treadmill

I went on a course for computers
It surprised even me, truth to tell
I'm really in debt to the tutors
They taught me quite quickly and well.

The time came to finish the classes
 Begin to do stuff on my own
Thank the fellow who'd got me my passes
And start my computing alone.

At first it behaved as it did at the school
And then by a strange twist of fate
My performance by then being really quite cool
It asked to perform an update

I only clicked twice for the questions it asked
As it worked on the new installations
It even successfully finished the task
And posted its congratulations

I tried to continue but couldn't, you see
For the things I relied on weren't there
The stuff on the screen now looked different to me
And I thought to myself "That's not fair"

It seems that I'm now using system mark four
This program is different and new
And I need to go back and study some more
But I don't think I'll bother, do you?

Retail Therapy

I'll treat myself, I think I may
Drive over to Brent Cross today
I'll take my car and find a spot
To leave it in the parking lot

I go to Fenwick's for a browse
My eye falls on a likely blouse
This blouse as far as I can see
Is just the thing I want for me

I think I'll have a closer look
And so I take it off the hook
I check the tag, the price is right
I think I'll buy it, yes I might

But first I have to try it on
That is a thing I'm strong upon
I go to where the lady's sitting
Outside the cubicle for fitting

I put it on. It suits me well
Quite fashionable, truth to tell
The lady says it's just the thing
But does that have a doubtful ring?

There really is no way of telling
Is she sincere, or is she selling?
I change my mind. Now I can see
It's really not the blouse for me

I take it off, replace my top
And leave to find another shop
John Lewis at the other end
And then I chance to see a friend

It's Pam. Long time no see my dear
How very nice. What brings you here?
How are your children? How's your cat?
You husband's left you? Pity, that.

There's Starbucks. Let's go in and drink
We need a tete-a-tete I think
Yes I was shopping, I concede
But this is what I really need

The Perils of reading

Dear occupier, what's your name?
Are you aware that you can claim?
Whether you've suffered hurt or not
We'll help you get an awful lot

That snack you've bought, it's lovely but
It might contain a trace of nut
The small print should be read with care
It's often neither true nor fair

The seller of the goods entices
The public with amazing prices
The cost is low, the value high
Exclusions, sadly, may apply

Those cars they're selling in the press
Go extra miles on less and less
This information could prove bad
On careful reading of the ad

As for a mortgage, keep away
Your home's in jeopardy, they say
If it's a peaceful life you're needing
The answer's simple: just stop reading.

A hacker's life is not a happy one

The jungle of the internet
With wolves and tigers is beset
Behind its bushes hackers lurk
Malign attackers are at work

The hacker's life's a lonely one
It's not an awful lot of fun
To find a mug and try to pick
His password by some devious trick

Or break his locks or find a door
That he forgot to shut before
And though a problem this may seem
You're aided by a great machine

For any code devised by man
Another one decipher can
While on occasion it is tough
You'll win if you try hard enough

And now you're in and safe on board
You'll surely merit a reward
Perhaps you'll try to have a bash
At getting to the victim's cash

You'll find it is a subtle art
To get him and his funds to part
And when arranging to collect
You must be very circumspect

For once you start a life of crime
You may end up by doing time
Perhaps you'd better end this run
Abandoning that line of fun

Now a successful hack you've tasted
How to ensure it isn't wasted?
One answer is, just let him know
And having done it let him go

Some hackers dump a load of trash
While others make computers crash
And some maliciously destroy
Computers simply to annoy

The truth is, and it's hard to see
Hackers are folk like you and me
And some start out by seeking fun
But end up sorry they've begun